Help..I'm in Love with my Abuser

Leaving the hurt for good

Written & lived by, Karolyn Kato Huddleston

The darkness of domestic violence, is far beyond the human minds capacity level. It's hard to imagine a person beating, kicking raping and degrading someone they claim to love so much. In most cases confusion is over whelming within each. Sometimes both parties are mentally broken and have issues with low self-esteem. When I was abused, I certainly did.

 I couldn't even talk to God.

Because to a certain degree, I blamed him for the situation. Not realizing, that I stepped in the darkness on my very own.

All the odds were against the relationship but I pushed and pushed until I got him in my life. Removing him from the lives of three other females.

I felt victorious when he moved in. It wasn't two weeks before he brutally beat me in my bedroom closet.

He was the first man to ever hit me. And I was totally lost as to what to do about it.

The Repetitive Cycle of Abuse

I continued to be abused for so many years after that. Not by him, but the men who came afterwards. And my life was a cycle of chaos, arguments and beatings.

My children were affected and changed because of my decisions and lack of self-worth. Which kept me in abusive relationships over many years.

This book is to help victims, learn about domestic violence. And safe ways to free yourself, from your abuser.

Understanding domestic violence

do·mes·tic vi·o·lence

NOUN

violent or aggressive behavior within
the home, typically involving the
violent abuse of a spouse or partner.
"police, social services, and
voluntary agencies are working
together to tackle domestic violence"

Allow me share with you what I
know personally, from living in it.
And watching the majority of
women I know go through it.

The abuser is like a predator, they wait for the moment to hurt you. They seem to enjoy manipulating their victims. I've seen so many abusers, smile while their demeaning and beating their victims.

Some people think domestic violence is totally physical. But it's so much more.

It's a control issue, that is needed within the person committing the act. For many reasons this person can be this way, and condone their behavior.

By saying things that always place blame on their victim. I will make a list of the things said.

Then ask yourself. Whether you've heard these lines over and over again.

1.) Look what you made me do

2.) You always get me way to upset

3.) If you'd do what I say

4.) Can you do anything without upsetting me

5.) You like pissing me off?

6.) It's your fault I hit you

7.) You made me do it

8.) I didn't want to do it, but you kept pushing me

9.) See, I knew you was going to take me there

10.)   Dam you always get me so

upset

11.)   I never act like that until you

come around

If you've heard even one of those lines.
Chances are your being abused mentally
and/or physically. And one is just as bad as
the other.

Abuse doesn't just start off extreme and
deadly. Most times it starts of gentle and
sweet, until the abuser snaps.

Or is put in a predicament, where they lash
out. Because usually the abuser has no other
coping skills.

So, the abuser uses their mental and physical
strength to break you down. So, that they
can be rewarded with the felling of control.

It's almost like a high to the abuser.

And with each confrontation, the situations

will get more violent. Meaning more deadly

to the victim.

The abuser's apology

Be careful when you are abused

because the abuser will manipulate

you constantly.

And sometimes the abusers best trick

is pity. Making themselves appear to

be the victim.

Seriously, they will want you to feel

like their pain is the cause for the

actions shown.

They will tell you sad stories about

their lives. They will make all the

attacks on you, be about them.

Be very cautious of this act. As the

abuser, is always a few steps ahead.

That you will never know what to

expect.

And the sad thing is, your abuser is

not smarter than you. They just

found a way to tap into your mind,

and manipulate. Usually through the

heart.

Realizing your abused

You will know that your abused the

first time he hit you.

However, most of us don't

acknowledge the seriousness of it. Or

leave immediately.

We're already in too deep with the

abuser.

We've been mentally and physically

taken over by the manipulator.

Feeling lost and embarrassed is the

feeling that washes over us, every

time he hurts us in any way. And it

becomes beyond difficult to share

our situation with anyone else.

And if we do share, were slow to act.

The red flags were waiving nonstop

from the beginning, but we ignore

them.

 Because we want to see the best in a

person that we're attracted to.

Remember, we're always on our best

behavior in the beginning of most

relationships.

But we must look deeper when
entertaining the thought of being
intimate with someone.

And I don't mean only sex, I'm
speaking of bringing someone new
around your children, family, work
place etc.

Because the minute you discover that
this woman or man is crazy, mean,
dangerous, or simply not the one.

You've already given them the
blueprint to your personal life.

But realizing that you are deeper into

a bad situation is the first step to

changing it.

This is no time to kick yourself. It's

time to think rationally, because in

domestic violent relationships.

Leaving can be a deadly situation for

the victim and those around them.

But, so can staying.

Preparing to leave safely

1.) Searching for help and resources

is a great start. But must be

carefully done. Computers and

phones keep track of all searches

and calls. And you don't want

your abuser discovering your

plan to leave.

So, you may want to use computers

at another place besides home.

Libraries or facilities that allow you

to use their computers. Also, you

may try using a friend, make up an

excuse that your computer isn't

working. Unless you trust them to know the details.

Another good idea is having a prepaid phone with minutes, at all times. This will assist you in your ability to make calls to agencies and people who may be able to help you. Without risking your abuser finding out.

2.) **Researching safe places**

Call around and look up as much as
you can about places to go. When
you leave, you will need this support
and safety net. Call around and find
out all types of information. Like,
where are their safe houses, and do
they help with legalities.

Do not be afraid to ask questions. No
question is stupid. This is a critical
situation and you are talking with
people who specialize in helping
victims of domestic violence.

If you have a difficult time finding

where to start, try the National

Hotline 1-800-799-7233 or The

Worldwide International Directory

of Domestic Violence Agencies.

These people can help you with

finding helpful resources, that can

get you the proper information

needed for your situation.

3.)Looking for actual locations

This will be helpful in helping you find the exact location of the place that will help you when you leave.

Knowing the destination is good but not a must. And remember don't google it from your phone or laptop. If not erased or very careful, it may be discovered by your abuser. And these places are kept very secure for the victims that come there. So, use caution about this information.

4.)Share with a person you trust

As victims, we normally seclude and become withdrawn. Due to embarrassment, fear and manipulation from the situation.

But it will be very helpful to have a trusted friend, family member, preacher or someone that can listen. As well as help you get out of this situation. You can share a plan with this person, and get much needed support now and for the actual departure.

Sharing your situation may take

some of the load off. And help you

focus on getting out of this situation.

Discuss having a secret code or way

of communication with them to. Just

in case things get escalated and you

contact them.

Be specific with your friend, let them

know exactly what you need from

them during this time. A ride, a place

to stay temporally or just support.

5.)Stashing a little cash

If you can stash a few dollars here and there. It doesn't have to be anything major. But every little bit does help.

Even change is great, loose change always adds up. And can come in handy when you leave.
This isn't a must, but may be helpful later.

6.)Packing a small get away bag

Packing a small bag is also helpful,

but you must be cautious with this

bag. It must be used for the most

important items.

Clothes for you and the children (if

you have children). Medications, or

medical papers.

A few small important things you

may want to keep, pics, jewelry etc.

Be sure to include, your important

documents. Such as driver's license,

I.D., social security cards, birth certificates, shot records for the kids, etc. nonperishable snacks, like cheese and crackers, jerky, juices etc.

Also, you may want to keep this bag at your trusted friends place, and retrieve it when you leave or afterwards.

7.)Keep an extra car key & prepaid phone

If you have a car, it may be wise to

keep in extra key hidden somewhere.

Just in case the abuser takes yours.

Or you can't get to your set.

Keeping a prepaid phone and an

extra key in your departure bag

would be a great idea.

The phone you could use for your

researching and phone calls after and

before leaving.

8.)**Planned destination**

Have a specific location to go to
when you leave. Whether it's your
friend's house, shelter or the police
station.

This is also important because when
you leave, you never know what the
situation might be at that time.
And being panicked, and unsure of
your plan, may lead you right back
home. And that can be deadly.

9.) **Leaving during a safe time**

Be sure to leave during a time that
you can safely get away. During a
time when your abuser is not coming
right back.

Like during their work hours or visits
to others.

But if the situation has escalated and
you're in danger. Call 911
immediately, the police will remove
you from the situation and home
upon request.

And be careful calling the police, do
so without the abuser knowing.

Call and leave the phone on, but

hidden, so 911 can hear what's going

on, give them the address when safe

to do so. Some cell phones don't

have your actual location available.

And whenever you find a chance to

call the police, always give location

first. Just in case you can't talk

again.

10.) **Go straight to your destination**

When you leave, go straight to your destination. Do not stray from your agenda.

Be cautious of being followed. And don't drive the familiar routes. And in case of tracking devices on your cell phone, you may want to use your prepaid cell phone.

This will be a very stressful and scary time for you. But don't give up. Remember, that this is a new beginning for your life and you will succeed. Stick to the program, and don't let anything send you back to the horror your leaving. And if you need any help please call the resources provided. They are trained and ready to help you move forward. And please feel free to join me on Facebook, Karolyn Kato Huddleston, Twitter, KatoKato120, Instagram, daddiesgirl127

National Domestic Violence Hotline

1-800-799-7233

Worldwide International Directory of

Domestic Violence Agencies

http://www.vachss.com/help_text/domestic_

violence_intl.html

Information and Statistics for domestic

violence

http://www.ncadv.org/

If you enjoyed the help from this book I have more that can share valuable information with you about love, relationships and abuse.

LIKE THESE>>>>

How to Make a Woman Melt (http://a.co/iUsWxaC)

How to Survive Heartbreak (http://a.co/0NcSrOR)

Loving Someone..That Don't Love You (http://a.co/dVxVwee)

So Flawed..Yet So Beautiful(http://a.co/022J3nl)

The Battle Within (http://a.co/4nyMG7j)

Phone Numbers and notes

Notes and agendas

www.ingramcontent.com/pod-product-compliance
Lightning Source LLC
LaVergne TN
LVHW020059190726

843498LV00012B/1898